The Art and The Tao

of

Helping

Those

Who

Need

Us

Joyce Ivory Lea

For the one who receives and
the one who gives
comfort and joy

Don't ask yourself what the world needs. Ask yourself, "What makes me come alive?" Then do that.
Because what this world needs is people who have come alive.
--Howard Thurman

Contents

Foreword
By Caroline McCullough

In their early twenties, Bill Lea and Joyce Ivory fell in love and were married. A year later, their son James was born. As to be expected, the couple was overjoyed.

Then, the unthinkable happened.

One night after celebrating Jimmy's birth with friends, Bill fell asleep at the wheel of his car, missed a sharp curve in the road, and crashed into the base of an old cement oil derrick. He was thrown from the car and his neck was broken. (Those were the days of no seat belts.)

From that night on Bill was paralyzed, and Joyce became his caregiver and advocate. With a newborn in hand, she was faced with a difficulty most of us couldn't fathom and with challenges that went on for almost three decades. Through it all, she gained a strength and gentleness that is visible today.

A seed (as Joyce calls it) planted during that first year and a half after Bill's accident has blossomed into this wonderful documentation of the insights Joyce gained throughout the decades of his care, especially those concerning the hesitation and awkwardness people often feel when visiting someone seriously ill. I can hear her telling wary visitors, "Just come. Just show up. Just be yourself. Your presence matters!"

In 1987 Joyce wrote a small quick-study guide, *Visiting the Ill, A New Art Form*,[1] which offered suggestions on how to create a more positive exchange between patient and visitor. In the present book, she expands on her ideas, goes deeper into the patient-visitor as well as patient-caregiver relationship, offers an abundance of *dos and don'ts*, and opens our eyes to the simple truth that by our presence we have the capacity to comfort and support a loved one in need.

Joyce openly shares her mistakes and her breakthroughs while taking care of her two children (joining the family twelve years later was a delightful adopted baby girl, Dorothy) and her quadriplegic husband.

Whether you are taking care of someone who is in the hospital or ill at home, who may be facing painful treatments or his own mortality, or whether you are a patient who would like to help guide your loved one's helping hands, you will find tips and valuable insights from someone who has much to share. Joyce writes in a kind, personable, and honest way.

---

[1] *Visiting the Ill, A New Art Form* was promoted by several hospitals in California and Utah. A study done at Cottonwood Hospital in Salt Lake City found that visitors who read the booklet prior to visiting their patients felt more at ease and the interactions with them were more beneficial.

A Note from the Editor

I met Joyce when she was 85. I had been in San Diego for less than a week when one of her friends asked if I would pick Joyce up and bring her to a New Year's Eve gathering to which we both had been invited. I agreed. The first thing I noticed was a bounce in her step, which I later discovered was due to her ongoing and excessive love of dancing, and a joy in her heart that seemed to choreograph her world as well as time itself. I felt she had known me all my life. From the very first moment she stepped into my car, a beautiful friendship has been blossoming. Joyce nourishes my heart, opens my mind, and teaches my spirit to dance.

It wasn't until I read the first draft of this book that Joyce and I spoke about the days surrounding her son's birth and her husband Bill's horrific accident, and of the twenty-six years she cared for him. What I learned from our talks is that the words written within these pages reflect the form they take in her being. She doesn't merely write ideas or suggestions; she breathes the essence of her life onto the page, inclusive of her wit and characteristic charm.

I didn't know Bill because he had died many years before Joyce and I met. But curiosity led me to rent *The Men*, a 1950 Marlon Brando movie in which he had had a bit part. When the camera began to follow the doctor on his rounds of a quadriplegic ward, I knew Bill's performance was soon approaching. What I wasn't prepared to see, however, was how young he was. Even though I was aware the accident happened when he was 23, somehow I expected him to look older, like he would look now, having been married for several decades. Of course, this was not a logical expectation. Bill was handsome, even vital, although he could demonstrate to the doctor his control of only a single finger.

This silver-screened image of the man moved me in ways I hadn't anticipated. I was struck by the intensity of shock and despair Bill and Joyce must have first experienced and of the enormity of the challenges that faced them. I realize now I was startled by these impressions because I couldn't find a trace of victim consciousness or of bitterness in Joyce. Indeed, the opposite is the case. Joyce is a cheerful woman who radiates kindheartedness and gratefulness.

This book captures all that Joyce has experienced, not only when caring for her husband, but in her years of service to so many others in need. The first ten chapters embody the wisdom of these years, giving us insight into the practical ways we can transform the most challenging of times into profound life-affirming opportunities. She ends with *Our*

Story. Here all the words of the chapters preceding it are fleshed out into their fullest human expression as we experience the valleys and peaks of her family's journey and witness the birth and formation of the art and the tao of helping those who need us.

I experienced Joyce's wisdom and sensitivity firsthand a few years ago when I was challenged by a physical and emotional trauma that proved difficult for both my friends and family to bear. Most kept their distance. But Joyce never wavered from showering me with constant, unconditional acceptance. She listened without judgment, and thus when she spoke, her words carried extraordinary weight. She would meet me in my own world without trying to remake that world or to convince me of what might have been her own perceptions or opinions. The healing effect was enormous, and I will always be indebted to Joyce for her perseverance and her kindness.

I am certain as you ponder the words that follow and fine-tune them to encompass your unique character and situation, you will find countless approaches to comforting the person in need in your life. And I promise that you too will be comforted.

--Michele Nadder

Introduction

Only two days after the birth of our first child, a car accident paralyzed my husband from the neck down. Our whole world changed. I felt helpless, our lives seemed overwhelming, and the road to renewal was either hidden from my view or seemed impossible to pass.

When I first visited Bill after the accident, I sat in a chair next to his bed waiting for him to stir and thought, "*Oh my God, what in the world has happened? What do I say to him? Will he remember we have a beautiful new baby? Will it make him cry if I start to cry?*" At first, I had mixed emotions. I was angry with him for falling asleep while driving home after celebrating our son's birth with his friends (perhaps celebrating a bit too much). I was also scared to death he was going to die. I didn't know what to say, or do, or not say and not do. I was weak and distraught. But not for long. Somehow, sitting there next to Bill's bed, something strong inside me crept silently through my body like melted honey.

It was a sense of calm and peace and when I looked up at him, I was simply grateful he was still with me.

My first words came easily, "Thank God you're alive."

Bill was sedated and semi-conscious, but I heard a whispered "Yes."

This unpredictable pattern of responses continued for years. Moments, days, or even months of overwhelming challenges could be eased and transformed by a newfound confidence or a meaningful acceptance of life's twists and turns or even a laughable appreciation of the absurd.

It is in looking back that I see much more clearly the multitude of positives that came our way. The greatest of these were our children and our families. While I was learning to take care of a quadriplegic, many kind and nurturing people would teach me about my own self-care. It was an ongoing dance. As a challenging situation arose, inevitably some kind of aid or assistance showed up, sometimes unrecognizable until later. "It's the long view," Bill would say, with tongue in check, while I was piecing together how that challenge had mellowed into a respectable solution.

And so it was that in the weeks and the months following the accident, I felt as if I was in a fog even though decisions were made and things got done. What Bill and I were learning was to simply take each step at a time. As unimaginable as it may seem, with each passing day, we learned to be more accepting of what was presently going on and to take care of the moment. Adapting was a key factor in moving forward. *It is what it is* became our mantra, and it helped to open our eyes to new possibilities. Bill's wit also saved us. When you live with someone who has a great sense of humor, and uses it, the world can go from black to white or from cold to warm. Humor was our secret for bringing us out of desperation. We laughed a lot, and yes, we cried some too.

While the pace of healing and moving forward sometimes seemed to be that of a turtle – and it often was, we discovered it didn't really matter. Having stumbled upon grace, I found there was something in our makeup, our human spirit, which made it possible to bear up under the most dire circumstances. Something nudged, pushed, and then poked us to make the best of our lives, even when the state of our affairs appeared to be stopped solid.

Bill's attitude grew more and more positive, and the courage of his determination became our anchor. He moved on from the first few years of wondering "Why me?" to experiencing a genuine acceptance of what he called his perfect part in this perfect universe.

I moved on from those first frightening and overwhelming feelings to looking for ways that would help improve both of our lives. As often as possible, I tried to keep my state of mind elevated and at ease. Fortunately, my mother was a "non-worrier" and many of her teachings had filtered into me.

I noticed that whenever I pulled myself into a higher outlook, our lives were enriched and felt easier.

There was a third factor in our relationship that also enriched our lives, and it really had nothing to do with our own efforts or insights. Our baby Jim and later our daughter Dorothy brought such joy and fun into our lives. Their enthusiasm and healing presence entertained and comforted us and naturally shifted our focus from what we couldn't do to the joys of raising a family.

Since the publication of *Visiting the Ill, A New Art Form*, I have been encouraged for almost three decades to write more of our story. I feel satisfied now having put into words the value and importance of assisting the ill and injured, especially by helping them to retain their dignity and to *start again*. It's my hope that the ideas and suggestions within these pages can help you to be present with your patient in a state of sensitivity and awareness so that together your lives will feel richer and fuller even amidst significant challenges.

Those of us who are closest to the ill or injured play a highly significant role in their lives, even though we may not realize it at the time. I didn't realize how central others and I were to my husband's well-being until I looked back to see what we had weathered together. His injury required me to become his advocate and his mainstay, at least until he became stable within his own condition. Once he was stable, it was time for me to give up the reigns. Bill was capable of choosing how he wanted to respond to new events.

Throughout the years, I've witnessed how people endure, standing up to meet their challenges as they weather unimaginably tough times. I've seen many rise out of hopelessness. And I believe their success came most often when the attitude of those around them changed from one of pity to that of empathy and support.

I saw quite soon after Bill's accident how important visitors were to his emotional state. Initially, he was extremely vulnerable to the ups and downs of those around him, and he fared best when people were optimistic, witty, and cheerful. I saw too that a visitor who brought even a tiny shred of comfort and encouragement lifted his spirits. As you might expect, the encouragement has to be authentic. We can't say, "You'll be up and around in no time at all," to someone who is not likely to ever be up and around. Yet we can say honestly, "I marvel at your patience," or "I'm glad to be here with you."

The Art and The Tao of Helping Those Who Need Us is the culmination of all that I learned in the twenty-six years of caring for my husband. Whether the time you spend with your patient lasts for an hour in a hospital room, or involves weeks of in-home care, you are welcome to follow, implement, and embellish my ideas as you search for the best way to accommodate your personal needs. Of course, it goes without saying that the art of a happy and healing relationship lies in the particulars of your own nature and of your singular situation.

With regard to the book, I've used the words ill, injured, sick, impaired, and the like interchangeably. And because the English language is limited, I've chosen to alternate the patient's gender from chapter to chapter. I've also tried not to impart heavy drama but instead to be honest about the challenges you may face.

What wells up for me is my thankfulness for the kindness and help we received. A startling amount of love was given to us by a host of people, from family and friends to hospital personnel and several remarkably gifted doctors. *Gratitude* is such a small word for all that it contains. It should be miles long because its meaning is so exquisite. It fills me even more now than it did then as it sinks in deeper, and I connect again with the magnificence of the "Givers" of this world. So many came our way.

In a small measure, this book is my way to pay it forward.

-- Joyce Ivory Lea

xiii

xiv

For him who has perception,
a mere sigh is enough.
For him who does not really heed,
a thousand explanations are not enough.
-- The Way of the Sufi, **Idries Shah**

SUPPORT

"I get tired of trying to listen to people who visit me when I can't even focus on where I've put my toothbrush. Help!" my friend barked out as I walked into her hospital room.

Listen to your patient

The patient you are visiting is likely to be upset, ill, in pain, and possibly terrified. Consider when we are hurting, feeling anxious, angry, or frightened. How well do we listen? For your loved one, listening can be an exhausting chore.

Thus, consider walking into his room with an attitude that you are going to be the listener. Without putting him in the role of host, allow your loved one to set the tone of your visit. It can be free-flowing as you give up your own agenda and dance to his tune. Just follow his lead. Be responsive. And of course, use your own good judgment.

Remember, when we walk in, we are a precious someone who cares personally about the injured one. Unless we are active caregivers, we're not there to give medications, to take blood samples, or to change his linens. We are a part of his personal life, and our visit can bring a sense of comfort – and even healing – during these difficult times. It can give our loved one a chance to relax, to talk about what he wants to express, or it can give us the opportunity to just sit quietly together without saying much at all. Even if he doesn't give clear indications that your visit is meaningful to him, know that it is.

Speak with empathy

The injured or ill are more likely to feel heard when we speak with empathy, the kind of concern in which we become focused and connected to what he must be feeling. Empathy is "to walk where he walks." How do we find his feelings? We can ask, "Are you sad?" He may nod, "No." We can ask again, "Are you scared?" We can tune into his world and feelings even if we muddle it some. Our job is to simply accept his answers while doing our best to connect with him. Our sincerity will show. And sincerity can make up for any unintended *mistakes.* Although we may not receive verbal acknowledgement of our sincerity, the open and honest goodwill behind our words will endure, even after the visit has ended. Have no expectations. To accept what he says is to stand up for him; it does not mean he will give you answers you'll understand.

Empathy is the identification of yourself with the other, a sharing of comparable feelings and motives that can help bring happiness to your loved one. This is something I had to learn especially at the beginning of my husband's time as a quadriplegic. Even though I had a lot to deal with, especially because his accident took place right after our son was born, I had to learn to be supportive, not only in actions but also in what I thought and spoke.

Empathy is actively listening to your patient with no judgments or critiques of your own. You listen with your whole body, with your entire attention focused on him. Empathy is being aware of and sensitive to his needs, thoughts, and experiences with an open mind and heart.

Sometimes while interacting with your patient, the frightened feeling he's having will be resolved. You can help him to consider new solutions or to find a greater strength and cheerfulness that will get him through his challenges. Your empathy and your understanding help your loved one to explore depths of his own being he might not have known existed. In addition, some health situations can improve significantly when a person clarifies and expresses what disturbs him.

Listen actively

As a patient speaks, giving him an "Uh huh," a "yes," or a nod of your head while maintaining eye contact communicates that you are listening, which further informs him of your interest and sincerity. Your active listening also has the stirring possibility of stimulating a flow of positive energy between you. Just listen, and accept whatever your own experience is of the visit, without worrying too much about it. We all dance to slightly different tunes, and you never know how much you are helping just by being there, attentive and listening.

Stay open to suggestions and listen for clues from the patient about what he expects of you or would hope to receive from you. You can start by asking:

"Is this a good time for me to visit you?"
"Is there anything in particular that I can help you with?"
"Would it disturb you if I . . .?"

We can also assist patients in learning to speak up and fend for themselves. It may be helpful to encourage your patient to ask for what he needs. My suggestion to my patient friend who had complained she was tired of trying to listen to visitors when she couldn't even focus on where she'd put her toothbrush was simply, "You can tell that person, 'I'm sorry, but I'm having trouble listening.'"

Maintain proper boundaries

Of course, don't expect that someone is going to necessarily follow through with even your *excellent* advice. It is important to keep in sync and to be with your patient. Just keep a light touch, offer your best, trust, and relax.

My quietly spoken mother, when terminally ill, rashly asked a chatty visitor to PLEASE leave her hospital room. Surprised by her unusual brashness, I squirmed as this incident was unfolding. But then I remembered how important it was for her to have quiet surroundings and was glad that she was asking for what she needed. Patients have boundaries, as we all do, and it is important for them to uphold them as best they can.

As a visitor or caregiver, you also have boundaries. Maintaining suitable boundaries is essential for both the patient and yourself. If he asks you to do something beyond your capability, you must honor your own limitations. Sometimes it may be necessary to say, "I'm sorry, I'm not able to do that for you," and suggest an alternate source of help, if possible.

Curb your curiosity (unless you've discovered it's wanted)

Because it can be painful or too private, it's better to avoid quizzing the patient or his family about personal details of his sickness or injury, unless they bring up the subject. Family members of critically ill people often deplore being asked, "Why?" or "How did it happen?" On the other hand, some family members may want to talk about it. Do your best to remain open and sensitive to how you can best serve each situation.

Often it is better to refrain from telling tales and giving comparisons about others in similar conditions, including, for example, your own illnesses, injuries, or operations. Let your intuition guide you in sharing what is most helpful for the patient and in refraining from what might unnecessarily agitate him.

It is also good to give positive support and to recognize your patient's potential to deal with his situation, no matter how limited that might be. This empowers him and enhances his dignity – two essential qualities for coping and healing.

A GOOD REMINDER is to expect the unexpected, and then to trust whatever happens during your visit. Whatever happens, happens. You can explore ways you might want to expand or improve your interaction with your patient, but remember to release yourself from any and all self-criticism.

Visiting and assisting the ill or injured can be riddled with areas in which we fumble and trip. But keep on. These people dearly need us, and the dance gets easier with practice.

An Aside

Before I was strong enough to drive after Jimmy's birth and Bill's accident, my father drove me to the hospital every morning. We'd go to the rear door where I'd get out of the car, into a wheelchair, up four floors in the elevator, and get back out of the wheelchair just so I could walk into Bill's room. Finally, one day my father stopped the car in front of the hospital and said kindly, "It's time for you to start to get your strength back." My response was, "I can't walk all the way to that front door – it's too far for me to walk. Too, too far."

My father gave me his well-thought-out reasons, and they made sense. I'd get weaker if I kept using the wheelchair, and it was really time for me to start to regain some of my strength. But, oh my gosh, it was a long walk on that sidewalk to that front door. I did it like a turtle. I got into the crowded elevator thinking, "No one in this elevator knows what a long walk it is to the front door." Of course, I made it to Bill's room, and I lived through it. My strength had come back because my father sensed when it was appropriate to give me that extra push. He had empowered me and given a well-needed boost to my dignity.

<u>TIPS</u>

- **Listen to your patient**
- **Speak with empathy**
- **Listen actively**
- **Curb your curiosity**
- **Maintain proper boundaries**

Patient And Caregiver Notes

*Optimism doesn't wait on facts,
it deals with possibilities.
Pessimism is a waste of time.*
-- Norman Cousins

UPLIFTMENT

"Ten minutes of great belly laughing gives me at least two hours of pain-free sleep," marveled Norman Cousins in his memoirs, *Anatomy of an Illness* and *The Healing Heart*. He went on to say that throughout two life-threatening illnesses, the magic factors that markedly improved his health, well-being, and outlook were hope, faith, joy, and laughter (That's quite a string of positives!).

Norman Cousins' insights into using the power of humor in his daily health regimen were validated. His physical condition responded immediately as vital signs improved. "Let's go for it," his doctor encouraged, and he supported Cousins by pulling together a daily routine that, along with the medical regimen, encompassed a large dose of old movie comedies such as the Marx Brothers films and television shows such as "Laugh In" and "Candid Camera." He also prescribed listening to amusing tapes throughout each day and into the night. Immersed in this joyful experiment, Cousins recuperated.

Laughter can help heal

A magnificent and brand-new art of healing had opened up to mankind. Just plain laughing could bring our bodies into better balance, better health. Whoopee! Something new was born that hadn't really been "scientifically" scrutinized or brought into the limelight. And it was so simple, so easy, so effective, so uplifting, and so much fun.

UCLA took on this newly introduced health protocol by doing a study on the connection between health and our positive emotions; Cousins was the principal researcher. I was excited to be included to work on this study and was privileged to be in his presence. He was a man who possessed both extraordinary insight and extraordinary wit.

I personally witnessed the effects of humor on the spinal cord injury ward at the VA Hospital in Long Beach, my husband's care facility. Patients here seemed to always be alive with humorous wisecracks about absolutely everything. Nothing was unmentionable. The men on the ward pulled a joke on Bill when he was new to the floor. One patient called out a number, and all those whose beds were within earshot laughed.

"What's so funny?" Bill asked.

Another patient explained, with tongue in cheek, "I'll clue you in. We hear our jokes so often that we've numbered them, each one, so that all we have to do now is to say the number of a particular joke, and we all know what joke it is. We get a laugh."

Ridiculous, of course, but was it? They were always pulling tricks on each other, being careful to leave those under the weather in peace. Eventually, all new patients, when they could handle it, got the *number* treatment. Once in a while someone would call out a number on the ward just to get a little rise.

I couldn't tell you if the health of these men improved because of their joking. No studies were done on the ward. But I can tell you that their spirits were lifted, in part by the joking itself, but mostly because of the sense of inclusion and belonging that laughter inspired.

Today, Cousins' pioneering work is cited in medical journals and by researchers assessing the impact of laughter on health. Studies affirm that laughter helps to improve the quality of life, especially for those suffering from chronic illnesses. As a result of these studies, many cancer wards across the country have incorporated laughter therapy into their treatment protocols.

So bring your positive supporting conversation into your patient's surroundings. As Johnny Mercer's long-ago hit song proclaimed, "You've got to accentuate the positive, eliminate the negative, latch on to the affirmative, and don't mess with Mr. In-between."

Dress up, not down

Consider wearing something that might stir your patient's spirits. My cousin Susan rummaged through her drawers and closets to find many of her mother's hand-me-downs (such as old hats, gloves, and some jewelry) so she could wear them each time she visited her seriously ill mother in the hospital. Her mother's first response was a smile. Then, as she began to recognize the parade of her own former items, she'd chuckle as soon as Susan walked into her room wearing the next old hat. Her physical crisis improved, and finally passed.

Similarly, when visiting my mother in the hospital, I wore a pair of high-heel Kelly green patent leather shoes that my mother thought was all the rage. I thought they would give her a lift. When I arrived, she was physically distressed and partially sedated, so I didn't mention my shoes. But when an aide started to help her turn over in bed, she glanced down at my feet, uttered the sweetest pleasurable sound, "Mmmmmmmmmm," and then whispered, "Oh, those beautiful shoes." This was the only uplifting moment I saw her have that entire day.

When Bill was hospitalized, I'd wear my newer, fresher, and more cheerful clothes when I'd visit, not my faded oldies.

He appreciated the efforts people made to dress well and would often acknowledge them. You can be natural, of course. Be yourself, and at the same time consider what might please your loved one.

An Aside

In their excellent book, *The Power of Two, Surviving Serious Illness with An Attitude & An Advocate*, Brian and Gerri Monaghan tell us they were treated with more consideration at their multiple medical appointments when they showed up dressed in their better clothes.

Keep surroundings clean and cheerful

Sometimes we're not actively conscious that we've been cheered by something in our surroundings, but we might recognize that we're breathing deeper, and perhaps have a bit more energy. When our eyes rest on order and beauty, rather than on a tray of dirty dishes, our bodies recognize the difference. It's as if a small spark ignites inside us when we experience something uplifting. This spark has the likely potential to enhance our health.

Besides his quadriplegia, my husband sometimes had a few days of minor illness at home requiring him to stay in bed. One of the ways I addressed these times was to clear off and wipe the tops of dressers, nightstands, whatever was there, and to tuck anything not essential out of sight. It always seemed to me that he breathed easier then. I'd even quietly marvel, *"There's a rush of fresh air in here now."*

There are subtleties in our lives that make us feel more at ease and that uplift us. For instance, I sleep better at night when I've opened my window. What are the small things that matter to you? What are they for your loved one?

I could usually depend on Bill, with his quick brand of humor, to bring a humorous witticism to an uncomfortable predicament to make it easier to handle. After hearing this sort of conversing at our home, my mother observed, "I like to walk in your door and hear someone laughing. You're very fortunate, you know." I knew.

We had good friends and family who laughed with us as we talked and played games – poker, bridge, checkers, chess, etc. And many times, as I'm sure happens to everyone, the ridiculous became sublime.

Give help and comfort

Another welcomed comfort is to touch, if that is what your patient likes. Some of us feel reassured by touch, but consider it may not be for everyone. Ask, if you're unsure. Some people like to have their feet rubbed. My mother liked to have her hair brushed with a hard bristle brush. If it is difficult for you to touch, be true to yourself.

When your patient is unable to do something that she could do in the past and wants to do it now, agitation levels can rise, even soar. It can be a difficult role in life to be dependent on others. Listening to her frustration helps. Letting her know you are willing to lend a hand also helps. Often doing a simple task, like putting a pair of glasses in its case, may be all that is needed in that moment. When you hear, "Oh, how liberating it is when my toothbrush is right where I can reach it," you know you've truly assisted.

This brings up the question: "What if I can't do what she wants me to do for her?" There are times when we cannot assist the patient, or any person, in the manner she wishes and so we must acknowledge our own limitations and say to ourselves, "This is not for me. Other arrangements must be made." Remember, it's good for us to know what we can do and also what we cannot do, while keeping in mind that new possibilities are always in the wings.

After Bill would undergo surgery, I'd usually spend that day sitting in his room while he slept off and on. I might read or knit, but my intention was to just be there and to keep the noise out. It was reminiscent for me of when my mother sat in my quiet hospital room after I had an appendectomy at thirteen. I still remember how secure I felt because of her presence.

We have a great deal to give just by our attendance. Our being there matters. Even with no conversation, we can still be a calming influence. Hospitals and care facilities are busy places. Just settling down into silence can be a soothing experience for both you and the one you are visiting.

Basic, simple incidents that occur between patients and their visitors (or caregivers) often touch us deeply and become enshrined in our hearts. Through the necessity of helping an ill or injured friend or loved one, we often experience a closeness not felt before. However, do not be disturbed if your encounter is entirely different.

There are as many ways to be inspired and uplifted as there are stars in the sky. We each have our favorites but keep your eye peeled for new ones. If you recall an inspiration that just passed you by, grab it back if you can. There are unexpected, sweet measures that happen around us that can give our lives, and our patients' lives, a lift. Be creative, cheerful, and peaceful. Bring in joyfulness and laughter at every invitation. A happy patient is more likely to recover.

An Aside

Sex is a personal thing. On Bill's ward, in the 1950s, I heard jokes, light-hearted comments while couples determined for themselves what was needed and what was best. Today, there are many organizations that address the importance and relevance of sexual intimacy.

The Christopher and Dana Reeve Foundation provides excellent information and how-to guides regarding treatment, suggestions, research material, protocols, etc. Its link is www.christopherreeve.org.

Help them to help themselves

There is an ever-growing understanding that when individuals contemplate their particular illness, they are better able to accept and overcome the limitations of their condition. As caring friends and family, we can help simply by realizing that our loved one has the extraordinary ability to ease some of her suffering. The key is an acceptance and an enhanced understanding of who she is and an appreciation that her potentials are often more than she typically realizes. I do not disregard the facts, but I do insist there are many unknown factors that remain unknown simply because we haven't yet discovered the *right* perspective.

<u>TIPS</u>

- **Laughter can help heal**
- **Keep surroundings cheerful**
- **Dress up, not down**
- **Give help and comfort**
- **Help them to help themselves**

Patient And Caregiver Notes

Joyce Ivory Lea

He drew a circle that shut me out
heretic, rebel, a thing to flout.
But love and I had the wit to win;
we drew a circle that took him in.
-- Outwitted, **Edwin Markham**

WHAT IF THE PATIENT DOESN'T WANT TO SEE YOU?

"I don't want anybody to come to see me. I'm a mess. I have nothing to offer anyone, and I want to be left alone. Please get it!" shouted Bert, a young quadriplegic, who lay in the bed next to Bill's.

Respect the patient's request

I shivered. Feeling unsettled with the commotion, I grabbed Bill's hand as I sat in the chair close to his bed. Hospital personnel, nodding their heads, stopped prodding the young man to let his family visit him and walked back to their offices, leaving him alone – or as alone as one can be on a ward with 24 beds. Bert rarely spoke to anyone, and within a few weeks he was moved to another hospital.

Four years later, as I was walking down one of the hospital corridors, a man with a big welcoming grin on his face walked up to me and said, "You don't know who I am, do you?"

I didn't for a moment, and then I saw that he was the angry young quadriplegic, Bert. I stood stunned, amazed and thrilled at his recovery. I knew some quadriplegics did recuperate to this extent, but it was rare.

A glitch of envy nudged me; I found myself wishing Bill's paralysis had healed to the same extent. Bert cleared the air with an explanation, "I want to thank your husband for my getting all this *return* because as I watched him and a few others, I was inspired. I thought if they can do all that work to get even a little return, I can probably do it too. So when I went to the next hospital, I started physical therapy and did everything that got me back upright and walking again. I had a lot of help. Please tell your husband, 'Thank you.'"

I did. Bill was as astounded and elated as I was about Bert's recovery. We knew he'd done an unimaginable amount of work to reach his new physical state.

This was one of those happily surprising shifts that come along, the kind that seem almost impossible. Keeping open to the unusual, even the miraculous, is worth a pound of platinum.

Be patient with your patient

Be as tolerant as you can with the person who doesn't want to see you. Perhaps he is reacting strongly to a dire physical problem. We don't know how a patient truly feels unless we're the patient, and sometimes even then it's cloudy. There are some patients who merely want to be left alone when they are not up to par. There are some who feel they look terrible and don't want anyone to see them, or it could just be that the timing is not right. No matter the reason, keep open-minded.

The same is true of the patient's primary caregiver (if it's not you). Whatever means you use in trying to reach the caregiver – sending a note, telephoning, or emailing – be gentle, as he or she usually has a tough time refusing requests.

Don't take "No" personally

If your friend or loved one doesn't want to see you, whether or not you understand why you are unwelcome, know that you have options. You could send him a note, an email, or a gift, or see if a short phone call might be welcomed. Most definitely, don't take "No" personally. There is no need to self-punish, and it's best to focus attention on what is most helpful for him.

Some spiritual and metaphysical philosophies state we don't need to be with someone to assist him, that our positive, loving thoughts and prayers can bring healing. If this rings true for you, send your loving thoughts and prayers. You may also wish to use some of the current healing methods such as Distant Healing Touch, Reiki, etc.

Encourage your patient to prepare visitors ahead of time

It can be helpful for a loved one, if he is able, to communicate his wishes about visits to his family and friends. My cousin Marilyn, when she needed an operation, notified a group of friends, her extended family, and her business associates about her scheduled surgery. She told them she didn't want visitors, flowers, or cards while she was in the hospital. She wanted to spend her hospital time as quietly as possible, believing that this would be the best way for her to recuperate. When she went home, she said that she'd welcome and happily look forward to their company and attention.

They adhered to her wishes, and when she was at home and stronger, she relished the company and gifts. This was a pre-planned "don't want to see you" event that culminated into a future fun goal for Marilyn and everyone else. This worked.

Sometimes it's OK to be unstoppable

Near the end of Bill's life, a long-time good friend asked to come and see him on several inconvenient occasions, and each time he called our answer was, "Not right now." Finally, Bill said, "Tell him to come and to please only stay a short time."

When our friend walked into Bill's room tenderly saying, "I know you don't need to see me, but I need to put my eyes on you – thanks for letting me come," I teared up, touched by his caring.

In this case, persistence made it work.

Whenever I'd phone my Aunt Ella to ask if I could spend some time with her, in a tiny weak voice she'd usually say, "I'm not very good today, Joyce."

I could hear *I don't think you'd better come today* on the tip of her tongue so I'd quickly offer, "I'll just stay a short time, all right?" The speed and character of my response were effective. She'd agree.

When she opened her apartment door and hugged me, I could feel her hands around me were like ice. I immediately got in sync with her by talking slowly, keeping my voice soft and my body movements slow. I felt as if everything about me changed. I was totally with her every word, her every movement. In a sense, I *merged* with her.

After a little while of holding her hands, she'd start to speak louder, and she'd seem stronger. We'd get around to family jokes that prompted mutual laughter. She had a wonderful sense of humor and I was so happy to laugh with her. As promised, I didn't stay long, but by the time I left, my heart and her hands were warm.

Most of us feel this way about some of the people in our lives. We'll do whatever it takes so we can be with them. We even become unstoppable in our search for how we're going to find the way to connect with them.

Trust your intuition; find the perfection

Trust your intuition. It's your #1 aid. Your creativity has no limitations.

If you are able to keep in mind that whatever is happening is in perfect order, you'll be looking at your situation from my husband's perspective – a perspective that touched and uplifted all who knew him.

<u>**TIPS**</u>

- **Respect the patient's request**
- **Be patient with your patient**
- **Don't take "No" personally**
- **Encourage your patient to prepare visitors ahead of time**
- **Sometimes it's OK to be unstoppable**
- **Trust your intuition; find the perfection**

Patient And Caregiver Notes

Gratitude unlocks the fullness of life.
It turns what we have
into enough and more.
It turns denial into acceptance,
chaos to order, confusion to clarity.
It can turn a meal into a feast,
a house into a home,
a stranger into a friend.
Gratitude makes sense of our past,
brings peace for today,
and creates a vision for tomorrow.
-- **Melody Beattie**

AN ESSENTIAL TIP FOR YOUR PATIENT

Ill, injured, and differently-abled individuals sometimes forget or neglect basic manners and need to be reminded of the importance of saying *Please* and *Thank you* to those who assist them. These are mutually beneficial terms. Generally, most of us haven't had any training on how to behave when ill. Once we have learned for ourselves the merit of our caring and sincerity and are no longer *expecting* gratitude, we can then encourage our patients to see the value of these basic manners. It is central to their well-being that they recognize the importance of showing gratitude for the care they receive. Your patient creates a circle of reciprocity as she responds to her benefactor. Consideration and appreciation are also significant because these traits display respect and recognition of those who are serving. Understandably, there are exceptions.

Consider the possibility that you may be the one who can assist your patient to become more aware of a kind and respectful interaction and see if you can find appropriate *gentle prods* or reminders.

Some suggestions:

"Even with your huge discomfort, how about trying to squeeze out a 'Thank you' when the aid brings in your dinner tray?"

"I really like it when you say 'Please' and 'Thanks' to me."

"I think I heard, 'Thank you.' I like that."

Several years after my husband's death I did some caregiving for a woman with cancer who was bedridden. She was heavily bossy while she kept me heavily busy with multiple chores, never showing a ripple of appreciation. My energy dropped quickly when I was with her. But when I found how tempted I was to linger in another room of her home where she couldn't see me, I knew our interaction was at a low level. Not a good feeling. So, I told her how difficult I found it to assist her when I felt disregarded. She listened, carefully in fact, and did try to be more considerate.

My friend Donna was summoned to her father's home when he came down with an illness and needed care. After two days of, "Help me!" "Get this!" "Do that!" and on and on, she said to him, "Dad, something is off here. How about a couple of *pleases* and *thank yous?*" He responded apologetically and easily regained his own natural manner of appreciation.

I have seen some incidents where demanding patients were ignored by the caregiving staff or given help only after the other patients had been taken care of. I wondered if this was the staff's way of saying, "Treat us better. Appreciate our assistance or we're out of sight.'"

Usually we function more effectively when we're in sync with one another. Those "in need" also need to give back or our interaction will be out of kilter. When both sides acknowledge each other – *giver* and *receiver* – they create a fulfilling bond. It's a natural circle of completion, an uplifting link for both. In some circumstances, a grateful nod is enough to form a lasting connection.

Patient And Caregiver Notes

The ultimate measure of a man
is not where he stands
in moments of comfort
and convenience,
but where he stands at times
of challenge and controversy.
-- Martin Luther King

WHEN TO END YOUR VISIT

"She'll be so alone if I leave, but I've got to go home. …I don't want her to think I've got something better to do. …What if she thinks I don't want to be with her?"

Getting comfortable with saying "Goodbye"

"Goodbye" may feel like a harsh word to say as you are leaving. Your loved one will be alone, and she may even seem lonesome or sad. Sometimes saying, "See you later" with a specified time and date can ease your departure. Or you may have just the *right words* and are comfortable saying them as you leave.

We must learn to ignore that inside voice, which nags us into getting overly concerned about how our patient will fare when we are not there.

In the beginning, I didn't want to leave Bill, and it was hard for me to say "Goodbye." Sometimes, after I'd pop back into his room to retrieve something I had left, I'd find Bill was already asleep. At other times, I'd find he had easily adjusted back into the hospital setting. My anxieties eased.

Most ill and injured people require a fair amount of quiet time to help them heal. Stillness can be a significant factor in their recuperation, and limits on socializing are often welcome.

This book is about raising your comfort level, both when you're with your loved one and when you're leaving her. The key to comfort is simple. When we are at ease ourselves, we bring this same sense of ease to our patient.

If your patient asks you to stay longer than you feel, "To thine own self be true." Don't run out of juice. There will be times when you won't be able to stay as long as she wants because of other demands on your time. It is essential that you respect your own needs also. You can firmly, and gently, state that you must go. Explanation? Yes. Apologies? No.

Our intuition is our best guide for conversation and for recognizing the timeliness of leaving our patient. Trust that when you leave, it is what she also needs. Like everything else in life, intuition needs practice. Act and check back later with her to see if you made the right decision. As long as you are honest in your efforts to serve both your loved ones and your own personal needs, intuition will develop.

There were times in leaving Bill when I didn't want to appear to be in a hurry, but I was. I had to put aside these interruptive and self-reprimanding thoughts that said, *"You shouldn't show you're in a hurry when you're leaving him, you know. It looks like you're anxious to go."*

I was anxious to go. It showed. And this was my best at that moment.

Even if you're leaving to do something fun, like going to a party, be authentic when you're asked about it. Hiding something makes conversation awkward and trying to protect your loved one from knowing about appealing events going on outside doesn't usually work.

Look for signs of fatigue

Become sensitive to your patient's "diminishing vigor." Watch for drooping eyelids or a weakening voice. Keep flexible. You may need to switch from a meaningful conversation to saying, "Goodbye."

When I was visiting my hospitalized former next-door neighbor and enjoying memories we'd shared, she suddenly changed the subject with, "I hope you won't get in too much traffic on your way home."

"Oops," I thought, *"she's sending me home,"* and, within minutes I was.

When to leave is a sensitive variable that is dependent on the circumstances. It's a time to tune into our intuition to get a feel for what our patient really wants and needs. My own experience is that most of us stay a bit past the time we should leave.

When our son Jimmy was born and a few days later Bill was in the hospital barely holding onto life, I had to spend two weeks in bed; other people took care of Bill, Jimmy, and me. I had many visitors because I needed a lot of support and at the same time, each one kept the visit short because I also needed to rest. Their visits were perfect.

On the other hand, twelve years later when we adopted our daughter Dorothy as a newborn, I enjoyed many people coming to our home to visit our new baby. I needed to rest then too especially because of my new regimen. Sometimes I lingered too long in conversation with my guests, and I would become annoyed with myself for not getting the rest I very much needed.

I'm sure this is why I presently advise not to overstay your visit with a new mother and baby.

We must not take it personally that our patient needs to have time alone. Give your loved one time to heal.

An Aside

In surveying many former hospitalized patients about how long they wanted their visitor to stay, the most popular span of time stated was "about twenty minutes with exceptions." Family members have their own time frame, yet no less sensitive.

I've heard nurses say, "The hardest part of my day is to take care of patients right after their visitors have gone because they're tired, edgy, and exhausted." A little less time spent with them can be a better choice than staying too long. Patients are often swamped with tests and hospital personnel.

Milton Erickson, a well-known psychiatrist and hypnotist who I was honored to know, found evidence supporting the nurses' perceptions that 'longer-than-needed' or 'burdensome' visits had taken their toll on the patients' health. As a hospital intern, he took vital signs of his patients prior to visitors and again after visitors left and found evidence of a downslide in these health indicators. Although well intentioned, visitors then did not know what you know now about length of stay and about appropriate and helpful ways to visit.

Give the patient time to heal alone

A beneficial visitor is one who can uplift the patient and who knows how to watch for signs that it's time to leave. You'll see what is best to do in your own situation. Keep alert to your patient's suggestions and ease her mind with the attitude, *There are no obligations here for me to host.*

What if your patient drops off to sleep? Again, don't take it personally. Be happy, even relieved she is getting some rest. Many "sleepers" have welcomed and appreciated the sense of being watched over as they slept.

As long as we are attentive and responsive to our loved one's needs, we will not negatively impact either their physical or emotional well-being.

Use your intuition for short or long visits

When my husband was hospitalized for a medical procedure, I'd usually stay with him for a couple of hours. In a more serious situation, like an operation, I'd be at the hospital for long hours; and if accommodations were available, I might stay overnight.

I liked being there. I felt I belonged, and I was comfortable offering Bill support, especially when I could take away the distractions that kept him from healing. Bill would let me know that he was happy I was there. If Bill had shown any signs indicating I should go, I would have gone.

He would sleep a lot at those times, and I usually had my knitting and a book with me. I was at home sitting by his bed while he slept and took pleasure in the silent joys of reading and knitting.

Remember your presence makes a difference

Those who are ill or injured contend with a much different world from ours. The constraints they experience can be overwhelming. By keeping yourself steady, yet flexible, you will find it easier to handle the multitude of unknowns that present themselves. Keep your sense of humor sharpened, laugh, and recognize the importance of your being there. You will gain immeasurable strength. I did.

Remember too that your presence makes a difference. You may never hear these words directly from your loved one, or from any other patient. Still, consider this as one of life's truisms even when proof is absent.

<u>**TIPS**</u>

- **Get comfortable with saying "Goodbye"**
- **Look for signs of fatigue**
- **Give the patient some time to heal alone**
- **Use your intuition for short or long visits**
- **Remember your presence makes a difference**

Patient And Caregiver Notes

GIFT SUGGESTIONS

Your presence is the most important gift you can give, yet there are also physical gifts that will help lift your patient's spirits, make his recovery time more pleasant and productive, and maybe even help him discover new interests.

One neighbor of mine shared, "Heart surgery is no easy thing to undergo, but the miracle of it is, because of that God-awful operation, my heart's OK now. And since I've come home from the hospital, I've been writing in a journal my wife gave me—actually putting into words the whole experience. I'm surprised at how uplifted I feel when I'm writing."

New authors sometimes come out of the woodwork after they've experienced the excitement of recounting a significant incident during their recovery, as new remembrances, appreciations, and lessons may come forth. Tools for expressing themselves through writing, such as journals or recording devices, can help open new avenues for your patient now and even after his recovery.

Electronics

So many electronic options are available today that were not available when I was taking care of Bill. If your friend or loved one is well enough to sit up, use of a computer device such as a laptop, electronic reading device, iPad stocked with his favorite music, portable DVD player with movies, or an iPad can help to give a wide variety of options for entertainment and support – the patient can play games, do some writing, read downloaded books, watch videos, listen to music and much more.

Most hospitals today have either cable or wireless Internet access available. This access allows patients to also keep in touch with friends and family, with tools such as Facebook, email, or Skype, and also allows them to keep up with their interests in current events. Such access can help make the difference between feeling cut off from the world or being involved with what is going on outside of the hospital or the recovery room.

Your patient may also want to look up information about his condition and can find blogs, articles, and forums with information and personal sharings from those who have dealt with similar health issues.

The Internet also allows you and others to sometimes visit your patient from the comfort of your own home. You may not be able to go to the hospital every morning or night to comfort him as he wakes up or goes to sleep, but you can check in via the Internet and give comfort this way. Skype even allows you to converse and 'be' with your loved one virtually, via a laptop or iPad webcam.

If your patient loves music, an iPod or MP3 player can give hours of peaceful relaxation and enjoyment – you can fill it with his favorite tunes, or give him a gift certificate to download music, films, or his favorite television shows from iTunes, Amazon, and other online stores.

Aside from electronic gifts are good old-fashioned gifts that can help inspire the patient or simply help him pass the time with some entertainment.

Books, Magazines, Games, and Notecards

- Most hospital gift shops have an excellent selection of **JOURNALS** for patients of all ages.
- **A MAGAZINE** about one of the patient's favorite subjects is often appreciated.

- **HUMOROUS BOOKS AND BOOKS OF JOKES** are welcomed gifts.

- **CROSSWORD PUZZLE BOOKS** are a popular way to spend quiet time for patients.

- Ask the patient if he has a **FAVORITE AUTHOR** or a **WISH LIST OF BOOKS** he wants to read.

- **NOTEPAPER, ALL-OCCASION CARDS, AND STAMPS** help to encourage the ill person to keep in touch and current.

Personal Touches

- **A SCRAPBOOK OF CARTOONS** is an appreciated gift that can be shared with others.

- A witty woman who wrote **AMUSING LIMERICKS** packed copies of her most cheerful ones into an attractive folder and took them to read to her patient, leaving the folder there so others could enjoy them.

- A psychiatric patient said her most enjoyable gift came from a visitor who brought **ARTISTS' TOOLS** and who then taught her a new, simple drawing technique.

- Our five-year-old son penciled a small matchstick sketch of his hospitalized father, and my husband kept the drawing in his bedroom nightstand drawer for years.

Personal Items

- **GIFTS OF GARMENTS – ROBES, BED SOCKS, BED JACKETS, A GOWN, OR PAJAMAS** can help to lift a patient's morale. Clothes or bedding from home can also give comfort.

- A **SMALL PILLOW** can come in handy as a back prop, or you can try a traveling **BLOW-UP PILLOW.**

The Unusual

Flowers and get-well cards are great. You can also try something a little different:

- A **BALLOON** or a **BALLOON BOUQUET** can add a cheerful touch to your patient's room.

- Send in **A CLOWN**. Silent clowns and mimes have been shown to be of tremendous therapeutic value. Can you think of a better listener?

- Bring in **A MUSICIAN** to play favorite tunes or peaceful music. Friends or family may also be able to cheer the patient up by playing music, reading, or offering other forms of entertainment.

Garden Goods and Food

- **FLOWERS AND PLANTS** represent health, beauty and life; however, we need to consider that some people have allergies and some hospitals have policies against such greenery. Check with the family and/or hospital.

- **FRUIT AND NUTS** can be welcomed gifts for patients to share. Check with the hospital first.

- **THE PATIENT'S FAVORITE FOOD**, if allowed, could get the most votes for favorite gift.

Your ingenuity and intuition will serve you in the matter of gift selection. Haven't you gone shopping to get a certain gift for someone, but excitedly found something far more appropriate?

The best gift and **THE MOST IMPORTANT ONE YOU CAN GIVE IS YOUR SELF.** Being there is the greatest expression of support and encouragement.

<u>**TIPS**</u>

- **Your Presence is the most important gift**

Other helpful gifts include:

- **Electronics**

- **Books, Magazines, Games, and Notecards**

- **Personal Touches**

- **Personal Items**

- **The Unusual**

- **Garden Goods and Food**

Suggested reading for you and/or your patient

Life After Life by Raymond Moody, MD

You Can Heal Your Life by Louise Hay

Love is Letting Go of Fear by Gerald Jampolsky

Love, Medicine, and Miracles by Bernie Siegel

My Voice Will Go With You by Milton Erickson, MD

The Power of Two – Surviving a Serious Illness with an Attitude and an Advocate by Brian and Gerri Monaghan

Patient And Caregiver Notes

Whether your duty is humble or great,
complete it with enthusiasm, with love
and with total absorption of mind.
-- Play of Consciousness, **Muktananda**

WHAT ELSE CAN YOU DO FOR YOUR PATIENT?

You've visited, kept in touch, and aided your patient in several ways. Now you'd like to offer something more.

Ask the family how you can help

The family can be in the midst of strained circumstances, perhaps worried and physically drained from traveling to and from the hospital or by caring for a loved one at home. Numerous, overwhelming details can crop up for the family or the caregiver and your assistance will be highly welcomed. When helping a patient or a family member in distress, remember to take deep breaths to settle down. This encourages them to do the same.

It is possible that at times no thanks will be forthcoming in response to your efforts and offerings. Again, don't feel unacknowledged and perhaps use this as a good time to remind all those concerned of the wonder and magic of a simple *thank you*. Remember too to take care of yourself.

Suggest how you can assist

This is a time when we have the opportunity to examine the treasure trove of gifts and qualities within ourselves. The old story about the only gift a juggler had to give was his juggling rings true. What special gifts can you give? Do you like to water plants, cook or sew, do yard work, or perhaps do laundry? Would you like to drive family members on errands or perform some of those errands for the family yourself?

These suggestions encompass patients who are recovering at home and those requiring ongoing care at home or at a facility.

Be creative

There are many creative ways to help. Housecleaning for the family or just "picking up" may be a welcomed aid to someone who is spending most of his or her time at a bedside. Consider taking the patient's children to the movies or out to eat. Perhaps offer to assist with correspondence, answer the home phone at specific times, or bring a casserole or a turkey; that is, after you've received an OK. One hospitalized mother said that the kindest gifts she received were those of food delivered to her family. She added, "Make sure no dishes need to be returned."

You can ask if any odd or small jobs need to be done. A little job can have a big effect. I liked it when someone short on time asked me if I had "some little chore" they could help me with because I could mention incidental items, such as, "I'm looking for a battery. Will you please hunt through these drawers to see if you can find one, put it in the flashlight, and get rid of the batteries that don't work?"

Our family was the recipient of countless helpful gestures. Once when we were new members in our community, several neighbors, whom we hadn't yet met, paid a surprise visit one Sunday afternoon. They arrived carrying shovels, trowels, pruning shears, and the like, with the message, "We're here to clean up your backyard." The yard had been unattended for several months before we moved in. The scene of all these wonderful people mowing, pruning, and digging up dead plants was heart-rending. We gratefully watched them restore – even manicure – our yard. We were thrilled to be the recipients of their kindness and to experience firsthand the truth of the platitude, "Many hands make light work."

Later on, we shared our newly painted shuffleboard court on the driveway with these neighbors, offering it to be "open year-round." It was our turn to enjoy the gratification of being the 'givers.'

Follow through

As best you can, follow through with whatever you have offered to do. If you pull weeds, dispose of them. If you start to set the table, complete it if possible. When I'd "pick up" where someone else left off, it could take me a while to see where to start. Bill's four siblings were remarkably good at starting and then carrying out the job. Completing a task relieves the family's seemingly endless tasks. It shortens their "to do" list and even lifts pressure from the patient.

Many of the people living in our communities are impaired in some way and need help. Giving is an aspect of our nature and our culture. It's necessary, although we don't usually know how necessary until we are in need.

When we are willing to be present and available for what is asked of us, we are not only responding to a need, but we are also acknowledging our shared humanity. Our flexibility and readiness confers worth and makes us of value.

If we offer what we can do and look for ways to be helpful, we "Cast [our] bread upon the water."

TIPS

- **Ask the family how you can help**
- **Suggest how you can assist**
- **Be creative**
- **Follow through**

Patient And Caregiver Notes

DIFFERENTLY-ABLED

"We don't want anyone to feel sorry for us," veterans in the Paralyzed Veterans Association remind us, both personally and in their literature. "What helps us most is for people to know we're just like everyone else. Physically handicapped people need special aids, but that doesn't make us strange or unlike other human beings."

Give empathy, not pity

To pity an individual detracts from that person's confidence and hope. It drains energy, and lessens her power and dignity. It infers that she is a victim. It also inhibits joy and the positive emotions that support well-being.

To empathize, on the other hand, offers respect and acknowledges that an individual has basic, yet remarkable qualities with which to handle her situation.

Differently-abled people usually recognize that their disability can make others feel uncomfortable and purposely avoid eye contact. We can help to remedy this by looking them in the eye and speaking first. We may be introduced to a couple where one is disabled. Address both equally, if possible. We tend to give the "able" individual the most immediate attention.

Children usually have no problem with this. They readily walked up to my husband to ask him why he was in a wheelchair. In a positive, clear and brief manner, he'd tell them that he had broken his neck in a car accident, which was why he was now paralysed.

When Bill's accounting clients came to our home office for the first time they were usually curious too, and Bill would give a brief explanation. This is not the same as quizzing the patient for details. Here the exchange, although direct, is honest and at its heart is a wish to elevate both parties to a comfortable ground for open communication. If you can help to empower your patient to answer appropriate personal questions comfortably, you will have helped him to learn an effective skill.

Empower patients to speak up

Individuals who are differently-abled must be careful not to lose the capacity to fend for themselves. Their circumstances leave them vulnerable to becoming an audience for those who might over-talk, over-stay, or be inappropriate. If possible, help your loved one learn how to speak up for herself. Encourage her to ask for what she wants. Suggest she can freely tell her visitors when she needs to sleep or wants a bathroom break. Most visitors will welcome this frankness.

On the other hand, many of those in wheelchairs or with any disability have a tough time and may feel awkward to allow another person to aid them. Yet we usually welcome the opportunity to be of use. It makes us feel good, even significant, to pick up the pen on the floor for someone who can't reach the floor. It is a natural reaction to be happy when we assist someone, especially when we give without any expectation of getting something back. This giving is *pure*. If you can help to empower your patient or differently-abled friend to speak up and ask for what she needs, you will create a natural bond between you that also provides her with an essential skill.

Listen without judgment

Patients are going through a lot and may wish to discuss or share some of their thoughts and experiences. Empathic, focused, non-judgmental listening – to the best of your ability

– will help you to tune into how your friend or loved one feels and help her to be more comfortable in expressing herself.

Most of us welcome someone who is willing to step into our shoes with us. By listening non-judgmentally, we create a greater possibility of interacting in a highly positive manner. Remember, no expectations. Whatever is, is.

Consider the power of humor and respect

I've already sung the praises of laughter. It is the best medicine in town. Always keep your sense of humor on the "ready."

Today there are many differently-abled men, women, and children. Veterans have some of the toughest circumstances that challenge them, their families, and their advocates. The simplest and most basic way of aiding these individuals is to listen to them, to keep as positive an environment as possible around them, and to treat everyone with respect and dignity. No "talking down," as if they're children. No patronizing. The solving of their challenges is a matter of a million possibilities.

<u>TIPS</u>

- **Give empathy, not pity**
- **Empower patients to speak up**
- **Listen without judgment**
- **Consider the power of humor and respect**

Patient And Caregiver Notes

<blockquote>
Man achieves fullness of being in fellowship,
in care for others. He expands his existence
by "bearing his fellow man's burden."
As we have said, "Animals are concerned
for their own needs; the degree of our
being human stands in direct proportion
to the degree in which we care for others."
-- Man, Mischel
</blockquote>

WHEN ILLNESS BECOMES CRITICAL

"Do you love me?" my aunt asked my uncle, as she lay in her hospital bed, near death.

"Yes, of course I do. Do you love me?" my uncle countered back, leaning over her fragile form so she could see him better.

Her answer, "Yes," closed the momentary tenderness as she dozed off with a smile on her face.

Theirs was a simple exchange, yet the words they'd spoken reflected a major switchover for two caring and kind people who had lived through an era that didn't seem to trade intimate and sensitive words easily. My heart did a little "whoopee" when I heard about this sweet occasion.

Stay flexible, open, and willing

We hear of extraordinary sessions between those near to death and their family and friends. Troubling matters often arise and dissolve; for example, someone might bring up the *other side* of a particular incident over which the *injured* party might have harbored resentment or sadness over his lifetime, and yet at this moment, he is willing to listen, even to reconsider his feelings.

Be open and agreeable to whatever comes along, for your patient and for yourself. Breathe deeply, and keep flexible. You can take a personal stance of willingness to be totally present. This willingness alone can help carry both of you through whatever is happening. It's not a time to place any judgments on yourself or your loved one. This is a prime time to tap into your own hunches, deep feeling, and intuition.

Tears and grief are OK. It's natural to feel sorrow.

A positive spirit can uplift the whole room

I felt privileged to be present with my friend Grace through her final moments. She was a woman who usually kept to herself and who enjoyed her solitude. A week before her death, we were talking in her room. I asked her, "Do you want to be alone?" "No," she answered. "I want people." I gathered several hospice volunteers who were close by and some of the residents from Grace's apartment complex. People began to chat and talk about different things. At one point in our conversation, someone answered a question about what she wanted in life by saying, "I'm looking for a man." Grace, who could barely open her eyes, said, "Me too." All our laughter filled the room.

Just before her death, a new person walked into Grace's room, a light-hearted man, a volunteer with Hospice, who made me laugh with a few humorous and clever comments. The whole atmosphere in the room shifted from being quiet and tentative to becoming light-hearted and uplifted.

The volunteer made a few more light and humorous comments, and I laughed some more. He did too. He said a few wittier things, and his eyes twinkled. I added a touch to it, as did my friend Donna, who was also there to support Grace. The three of us kept on laughing. My intention was to support Grace in her final moments, and we did, but not in quietude, as I had originally anticipated. My support reflected the change in her and came in the form of laughter.

As the volunteer left, we saw that Grace's breath was slowing down. She stopped breathing a short time later. Although we felt sad, Donna and I also felt as if a refreshing breeze had drifted through the entire room and given Grace a sweet and delightful way to pass on.

Let your patient set the tone

If your loved one is quiet, you can adopt his pose, and just be there with him, even if he sleeps. If he cries, let him. It may turn your own tears on – let it. If appropriate, you can make eye contact or hold hands. Breathing in sync with your patient's breathing can be comforting for you and also for him. Open to the possibility that you can both feel a caring connection, and let everything be just what it is.

Perhaps your loved one will want to talk about death. If you're uncomfortable with the subject, honestly tell him, but bear in mind these conversations have a capacity to help him and also to free you from your own old hesitant patterns.

Spiritual author Ram Dass provides a needed insight. "Remember," he writes, "that people near death have reached an expansive time. It's not a 'fold up your tent' situation. It's a time of readiness to open up. Pray for expansion for those who have reached this date with their destiny."

Whether this rings a bell for you or not, it is possible to take a stand for your loved one, a stand that will enable his particular experience of death to be a gratifying one. What more can we do for those we care for? Everyone has his own way of departing. Let it unfold.

Bring natural comfort to the dying and yourself

Howard Thurman gives this advice:

"Don't ask yourself what the world needs. Ask yourself, 'What makes me come alive?' Then do that. Because what this world needs are people who have come alive."

It is important to feel free to do whatever feels right. Ultimately, there are no rights or wrongs.

Being with a gravely ill person can be a time of great expansion for those in attendance. Even if you think you would find the encounter awkward, persevere if possible, particularly if it is someone close to you. Many people who have been with loved ones at their time of life-ending have claimed profound positive changes occurred in themselves during the vigil and even afterwards.

I experienced countless internal changes through Bill's last challenge of cancer. I'd grown from a sense of, "How will we ever get along without him," to a deep settled feeling that it was his time to go, and that we were going to be all right.

Bill also had the sense that everything was going to be all right.

It wasn't always like this however. After the doctors told us that nothing more could be done, we knew Bill's end was coming. I ventured into a search for new ideas. I went to the beach with a pad of paper, and asked, "What can I do for him, and for me, that I haven't done before?" As words and ideas sprang up I wrote them down. Some ideas were serious, some much less so: "Play tennis more, go to Church more, seek spiritual help." After reviewing the list, I circled "spiritual help." I began to read everything in sight…anything that anyone would recommend. In the end, in the year before his death, and because my readings were giving me a higher and sweeter viewpoint of life, the way I interacted with Bill was gradually changing. I was more patient; I had a greater capacity to do necessary chores; and my attitude toward life became more gracious and grateful. In short, I was more comfortably myself than I had ever been before. Bill and I had always been in love, but in this final year, our relationship reached new depths. By being true to myself, I was also true to Bill and to my family.

It was his time now to "go forward." We shed tears as we talked and watched him slowly slip out and "leave." When Bill died, between our tears I think we all felt relief for his release from his physical limitations and from every other challenge he lived with for twenty-six years as a quadriplegic. He'd had an exceptionally full life and we'd all been a part of helping him be the person he was capable of being.

A little later I called the rectory and two priests came to give final rites. That night, Dorothy asked if we could sleep in Daddy's bed. And we did. It was exactly where we wanted to be.

Suggested reading for you and/or your patient

On Death and Dying **by Elizabeth Kubler-Ross**

Still Here: Embracing Aging, Changing and Dying **by Ram Dass**

<u>TIPS</u>

- *Stay flexible, open, and willing*
- *A positive spirit can uplift the whole room*
- *Let your patient set the tone*
- *Bring comfort to the dying and yourself*

Patient And Caregiver Notes

*Live every moment
as though you were
building a temple.*
-- Thoughts, **Sri Ram**

TIPS TO STAY GROUNDED

Regardless of your patient's condition, your ability to stay grounded and balanced is valuable to both you and her. Uncommon situations can arise when assisting or visiting the ill. You may start feeling uncomfortable, tired, or unfocused.

These are a few tips to help you stay steady and alert so you can have helpful and happy visits with your loved one.

To keep centered (remember that everyone has their own time-table to get the effect needed):

• Breathe deeply – reminding yourself to do it often. One way is to swing your arms straight up above your head while breathing in and while you slowly lower your arms breathe out. Do this several times.

- Curl your fingers, then straighten out and stretch fingers several times

- Curl your toes, then stiffen them out several times. Get the sensation that you feel your feet.

- Plant your feet on the floor, with arms and legs uncrossed.

- Say or think of a word, a mantra, such as "Peace," and keep repeating it as you breathe (silently is ok).

- Do yoga stretches and exercises such as Tai Chi and Qigong to bring comfort and relaxation to your body.

The most important way to ground yourself is to create the time and space in which you can step out of the discomfort of the situation and embrace who you are. Allow every feeling and thought simply to be without judgment: every fear, every kindness, every desire to escape or to be somewhere else, every tear. Confidence and peace will once again be yours.

Our story is next and I invite you to read it.

Patient And Caregiver Notes

92

OUR STORY

I first met Bill at a high school prom at a country club near the beach on Sunset Boulevard. I was a petite, blue-eyed seventeen-year-old girl with long chestnut colored hair who easily recognized she was meeting someone sharp, witty, and with great rhythm.

 Bill, a blue-eyed young man with dark wavy hair, was a classmate of my escort that evening who told me, "He's new at school – just moved to Los Angeles from the East Coast, and I like him, but he's a little far out. No matter how much we razz him, he still wears a perfectly knotted tie to school every single day. He says, 'It's New York style.'"

Bill and I danced together a few times that night, and while the

tempo was
perfect, we
didn't begin
seeing each
other as a couple
until two years
later. We did,
however,

become good friends in the interim.

We married in our early twenties.

A sweet tender event occurred the following year when
our son, James William – named after his two grandfathers –

was born. Bill was
our blessed event
word out to nearly
Two days later,
at the hospital with
Bill went "a-
deliver the good
friends.

so overjoyed with
that he got the
everyone in town.
after checking in
Jimmy and me,
visiting" again to
news to additional

On his way home that night, he fell asleep at the wheel.
He missed a curve in the road and crashed into the base of an
oil derrick. The impact threw him from the car and broke his
neck.

From that night on, Bill was a quadriplegic.

The next morning after the accident I could not begin to fathom what my father was telling me. The information was too unwelcome, too unbearable to hear. I could only keep shaking my head, "No." I was confined to bed at that point, and with a new baby in my care, I felt helpless.

"Can I call him at the hospital?" I asked my mother, who had come to sit at my bedside.

"Not now, darling," she said. "He's too sedated."

The following day my father was driving Jimmy and me home from the hospital when I asked hopefully, "Could we possibly go visit Bill later today, Dad?"

"Of course," my father said as we turned into the driveway of my parents' home.

That visit never transpired. I fainted soon after stepping through my parents' front door. Two life-changing events had struck me almost simultaneously. One was practically the happiest news that could happen to a young woman; the other was about the worst news imaginable. The shock of it had virtually drained my body of all life and my mind of all energy.

I remained in my bed for two weeks after that. It took all the willpower I could muster just to nurse and care for Jimmy. I called him "Mr. Comfort" as his sweet presence uplifted me.

I see the birth of a child as something to be treasured and savored. I wondered sometimes if Jimmy was getting his share of "cherishing" from me, because I'd nursed him, felt comforted, and then melted into tears. I still carry a bit of that concern.

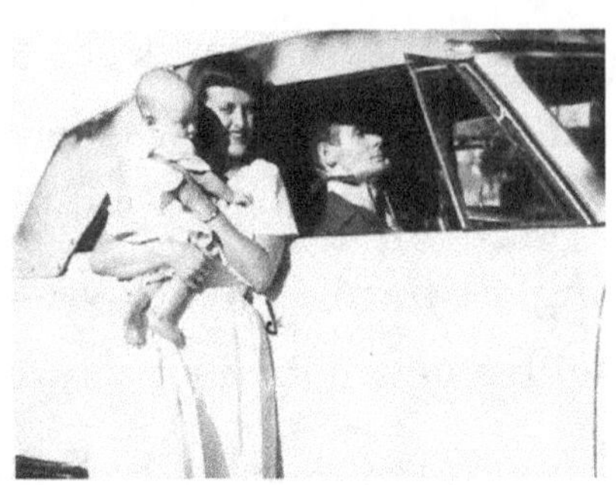

I seemed to have been enshrouded in fog for those two weeks. It was as if everything in my life had been churned and turned upside down. Instead of taking charge of even the slightest task, I simply gave up. It seems odd, but it's true. I wrapped myself in a blanket and curled up in bed, but not before saying, "Thank God Bill is alive."

Bill's family and mine joined forces to care for the three of us. They did the shopping and prepared meals, cleaned the house, did the washing, and waited on Jimmy and me. They

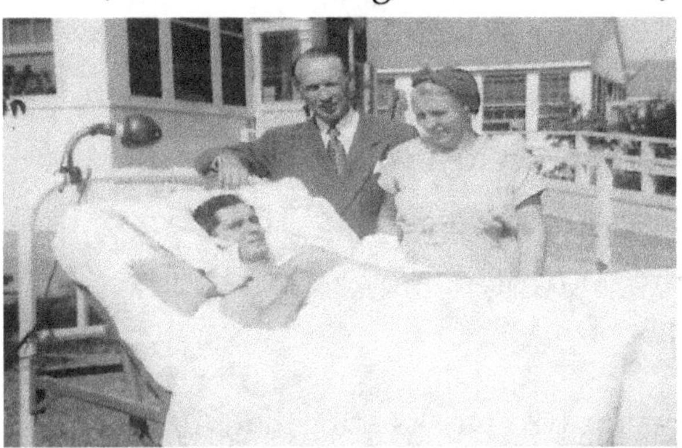

also kept a vigil at Bill's bedside.

Above the fog, I was a new mother showing off her precious son. Several friends and relatives came to my bedroom for short visits with Jimmy and me. A few people left messages on the phone and others sent comforting notes – each one reaching out to console us. Flowers came with treasured remarks. One such bouquet arrived with a message that reached into my core, as it was a reflection of Bill's favorite pastime. Written neatly on a small white card, it asked, "Does the little fellow play bridge yet?" It had been sent by one of Bill's bridge buddies.

Bill's healthy, vibrant nature helped significantly in saving his life. But his body had suffered a terrible blow. He lingered near death off and on for nearly three months after his accident. Eventually, he was moved to a veterans hospital and was placed under the care of two doctors renowned the world over for their cutting- edge work in spinal cord disorders.

Bill became more stable under their care. In turn, his rehabilitation regimen was stepped up. His therapy included swimming pool workouts, exercise in the rehab gym, and practice with his new-style fork so he could, without assistance, pick a cube of meat from a plate and place it in his mouth.

Around this same time, a motion picture company was using the VA hospital as a backdrop for a movie entitled *The Men*. It was a film-first for an up-and-coming young stage actor, Marlon Brando, who spent a full month, day and night, living on Bill's ward. Marlon Brando totally enmeshed himself in the life of being a paraplegic, and then played the part expertly, according to the critics. Bill

landed a bit part in the film as "Walter," a quadriplegic who could just barely move his fingers, which was true at that time.

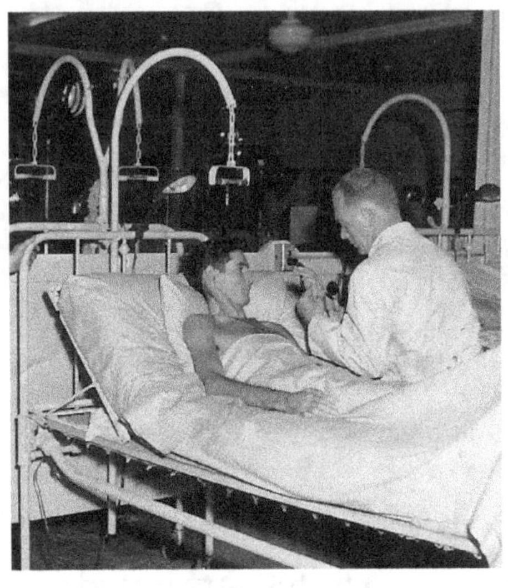

I was standing on the sidelines watching when they filmed the "Walter" scene, fascinated by all the props, the cameras, and all the detail that went into this small "bit." They had even put light blue sheets on the beds. Apparently, this shade of blue films a brighter white when compared to the screen appearance of a white sheet.

As the camera was filming the man in the bed ahead of Bill's, I saw Bill slump down slightly from his sitting-in-bed position. His face seemed to pale, and he had a pitiful expression on it. Something was wrong with Bill, very wrong. I wondered, "Should I stop the filming?" He looked horribly emaciated, and so suddenly. I didn't know what to do. The camera came to Bill and he played his small part, answering the doctor's question, "Well, Walter, how are you today?"

"I don't know, better I guess," he answered weakly.

After a few more words of dialogue and Bill demonstrating how he could move his fingers, the producer called out, "Cut."

I rushed to Bill's side, "What's the matter with you? What's wrong?"

He looked at me, surprised. Then in full control, and with a glowing grin, he said "Nothing's wrong. I'm an actor. I'm acting."

He got a paycheck for his part.

Several months later Bill and I, along with others from the hospital who had been actors in *The Men,* were invited to a gala opening of the motion picture at the Carthay Circle Theatre on Wilshire Boulevard. A fifty-foot bright red carpet was laid out at the entrance. Many wheelchairs rolled into the theater on that long red carpet with us that night and watched the premiere of Marlon Brando in *The Men* together. As I look back at this unusual turn of events, I'm struck by the mysterious and unpredictable nature of our lives. From one day to the next, nothing was certain. Yet so much was possible.

Nine months after the accident, Bill's doctor gave us a simple but profound prognosis, "It doesn't appear as if Bill will ever develop the necessary dexterity to even knot a tie."

I shivered, "Oh my God."

Those were tough words to hear, even tougher to absorb. I couldn't accept that this shocking catastrophe was happening to us. What had happened to my darling, my husband, my best dance partner?

As I tried to deny the doctor's comment, Bill shook his head, "That's a blow, doc. I'm pretty particular about my tie knot." He could, and usually did, make me chuckle.

In an instant, my mind had leapt from fear to gratitude as I thought once again, "Thank God, you're alive." I was learning how to honor whatever life would bring – perhaps not yet fully consciously – and to see order in the flux, a perception Bill had long understood.

Over the next few months, Bill was allowed to come home for longer and longer periods of time. I began to appreciate what it was like to have my own family, an extended family at that. We were living with my parents and younger brother. When Bill finally came home for good everybody pitched in to help him acclimate to his new surroundings. Back then there were no motorized wheelchairs, and only a few floor ramps, or wide hallways and doorways. We simply maneuvered his wheelchair the best we could, which, more often than we had anticipated, gouged countless walls and doorjambs.

Out of necessity, I went back to my former job as a secretary in the legal department of Twentieth Century Fox. By then my life had been so transformed that at times I'd find myself typing a legal document and sighing at the overwhelming magnitude of it all. I was working, had a newborn baby and a husband who needed to be dressed and undressed, lifted into and out of bed into a wheelchair and out . . . to be waited on endlessly. Thank God, I had a father, mother, and brother at home to help and in-laws who were kind and generous. I had read about people who overcame unrelenting stress and tension and in so doing had arrived at a higher level of consciousness. I hoped that would happen to me. And why not, I thought, "Anything is possible." I was already doing things I once thought were impossible for me to do.

I stayed open to "help," and was willing to embrace new opportunities that my doctor suggested. One suggestion was to meet with Dr. Milton Erickson, a well-known and respected psychiatrist. I drove from Los Angeles to Phoenix to see him, and Bill came with me. Dr. Erickson worked from his home, a large wood-frame house with six steps up to a lengthy porch. Three of his seven children brought Bill up the steps in his wheelchair, step by step, onto the porch where Dr. Erickson waited for me. Bill chose not to have any sessions with him. He had his own battery of doctors with whom he was satisfied, but I was soon glad to gain his counsel.

Dr. Erickson's office was dimly lit and quiet. Family noises didn't seep in easily. The doctor was known for his "teaching tales," which are what I recollect from our sessions. I was propelled to think about how a particular tale related to me. I found that each story contained many helpful and healing messages, some obvious, and some hidden. Dr. Erickson's theory proposed that although I knew the messages myself, I didn't know I knew them. My "job" was to uncover them.

He was an outstanding observer. I think he knew me before I reached the top step of his porch. The sessions were a mixture of helpfulness and puzzlement that kept "going on" inside me for months afterwards. I knew I had climbed up several steps of learning, because I began to recognize and to better care for my own needs.

An important consequence of our visit with Dr. Erickson was that Bill and I understood we could fend all right by ourselves for a few days with just a little assistance in lifting. The manager of our motel had graciously given that assistance.

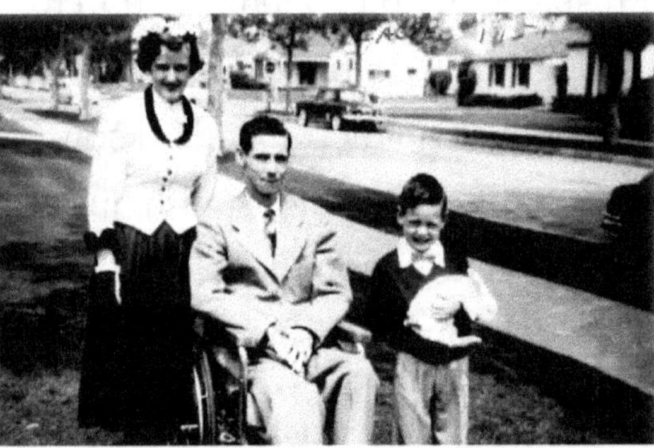

Still, I was envious of our friends who seemed so hearty, friends without disabilities, friends who were getting married, having babies, starting careers. I had no such dreams. Notions of career weren't even in my thinking. I was still living with my parents.

Fortunately, there was something about the way I was raised, something that was burned deep within me that said, "My friends are no happier than I am. They don't seem to be aware of how fortunate they are. Even if Bill hadn't been felled by an accident, I might have found something else to grouse about. And I do have a husband, a son, a family, and a home that I love. I'm really quite grateful."

This realization lessened a lot of my despair and envy. I fared better and sidestepped quite a lot of muck.

Bill and I began to socialize more, playing bridge sometimes at friends' homes or at my parents' (our) home. My father, too, relished sitting in on a hand when one of us wanted a break. I felt a sense of continuity and of belonging to something bigger than myself. I remembered when I was ten years old and my father would take me with him when he played duplicate bridge in large gatherings in the "card room" of an enormous theatre in Boston, my birthplace. I was not to talk when I checked in with him between the movies I had been watching. And between bridge games, he would check on me. These simple gestures assured each of us of the other's well-being and of our mutual love.

My father had a happy gleam in his eyes whenever he was sitting at a bridge table. Later, I saw that same happy gleam in my husband's eyes when he played bridge. Indeed, years before his accident, Bill had found it challenging to attend his college classes when bridge games beckoned on the campus.

One social event we both cherished was a result of Bill's acting debut. We were invited to the wedding of Stanley Kramer, the producer of *The Men*. In another twist of fate, Bill had dated Stanley Kramer's 'wife-to-be' when he was just out of high school, attending USC for a short time. The wedding was a dazzling event at the Beverly Hills Hotel, and it was fun for us to be around that crowd again.

We'd also go to the beach once in a while with little Jimmy and Bill's three sisters and brother. No wheelchair here. We'd carry Bill, each of us taking a limb, carrying him from the car across the sand to lie on a blanket – a fair distance from the rising tide – and then reverse the procedure to get back up to the car. He'd let us carry him, and he'd pretend that we knew how. While we tried to be careful, we often pulled and tugged on him in ways that must have been uncomfortable. Yet Bill quietly bore the "indignities" of our learning curve.

As the doctor had told us, Bill's potential for recovery wasn't great. He progressed to where he could slowly raise his arms and move the fingers of his right hand, and finally

even write – albeit, at a slower pace. Amazingly, his penmanship was almost the same as before he was injured. With great effort at first, he managed to keep a phone at his ear. His left hand was virtually useless, except for bracing the mug he could hold in his right hand. He required hands-on assistance for everything else, like getting dressed, bathing, tying his shoelaces, and transferring from his bed to his wheelchair and back again, and so on.

With careful and exact instructions, he taught me how to knot his tie.

The care Bill required seemed to be non-stop and around the clock. He was keenly aware of this, and he aided those who assisted him in any way he could. His ongoing self-discipline was a mainstay for all of us. I remember some of the philosophical ideals he embraced. For a time, he had studied with Jesuit Priests, and I felt that he'd been enriched by their brilliance and by their outreaching approach to life. Those three years of training, along with our support of his natural abilities, appeared to give him a sense of responsibility for his life. His own view of existence was consistently upbeat and people liked to be with him. His attitude towards himself and others was remarkably open, so much so that it took only a few years before Bill was consistently comfortable wherever he, or we were. I always said, "He just thinks higher and clearer." I often wondered if Bill's deep observations of life came from his Jesuit studies, although even when I first met him (before his Jesuit training had begun), Bill possessed greater insights into life and human behavior than those around him. He believed that the universe – and everything within it – is perfect. All life rotated perfectly; there were no jagged edges. This enlightened perspective existed in Bill even when his circumstances appeared dire, circumstances that would challenge the rest of us. He didn't talk about the Jesuit principals. I'd say he simply lived them.

Bill and I necessarily spent a lot of time together, and we came to know one another fully. His quick wit, and my appreciation of it, saw us through some significantly difficult times. He had the singular ability to make me laugh even as I was crying.

Of course, all was not work with Bill. Under my father's gentle eye, Bill learned how to handicap horse races. Before a big race at Santa Anita or Hollywood Park, my father and Bill were pictures of contentment as they sat shoulder-to-shoulder at the dining room table digesting every bit of what the daily racing form had to offer. They shared a multitude of similar interests, including music, mathematics, and bridge. Not least of which was the horserace.

Bill also enjoyed a budding friendship with my younger brother Billy who, at the time, hadn't been much of a student. With Bill's encouragement and mentoring, brother Billy rejoined the school system in junior college, graduated, and went on to UCLA. As a grateful graduate, he thanked Bill for his encouragement and instruction and in a short time my brother had become a successful stockbroker.

A welcome turn of events came our way, prompting me to throw my hat over the wall: I resigned my job at Fox Studios in order to drive my husband to UCLA and to serve as his note-taker. Bill had applied to go back to college and was accepted under the GI Bill. He was given a small stipend in addition to having his tuition paid in full. Hooray! There really were possibilities, even new dimensions for us. Going back to school was an absolute triumph. I literally sang from the rooftops. I was so happy and so deeply grateful.

Did I consider attending too? No, accounting was not my field, even though I'd graduated in business from Woodbury University. The gift of his continued education was not just for Bill alone. It was mine as well. Together we were going out, exploring a new world populated with new ideas and new people. I was thrilled. How much more could my plate hold? I listened to the lectures, and I took notes (he took his own tests and wrote his own reports) while I also took care of all his other needs. And I made sure that my needs and wishes were not ignored. On the contrary, at this point they were being fulfilled. Life was full, not just Bill's or mine, but our life. Perhaps I felt the way I did because I had grown and had gained an appreciation that everything is a matter of perspective. I could see this everywhere. A case in point: one of little Jimmy's playmates had told his friends about his own Dad's success at building a high tower of blocks that wouldn't crash. Jimmy proudly chimed in, "My Dad studies harder than anybody in the world."

We were scaling heights and reaching new dimensions that I never thought would have been possible, at least the old me would have been surprised. But in learning to accept the flow of life as Bill had been doing all along, I came to appreciate the immense potential in life's events, as it was no longer hidden from my view. Shortly after Bill finished college, we moved into our own home. My family had given us their blessing, though their faces revealed they were unsure if we'd be able to make it without their assistance. Honestly, I wasn't sure either, but it was time – past time really. In accepting life's flow, I could begin to trust that I would find needed resources either within myself or from others. Somewhere between independence and dependence lies self-reliance, a state in which I could be equally comfortable on my own or in asking for help when it was needed. Both my mother and father's goodbye words were, "You can always come back, you know."

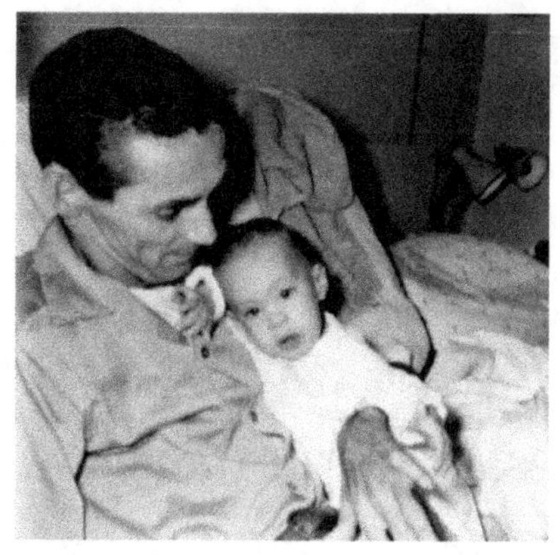

Twelve years after Bill's accident, we experienced a new tender event in our lives when we adopted a baby girl, bringing her to our home right from the hospital. Our daughter, Dorothy Maurine, named after Bill's sister and my cousin (whose husband had delivered her) was a super petite five-pound, adorable baby. By two, she had chosen Bill's lap (when he was sitting in his wheelchair) as her favorite place to sit.

If Bill was at a low ebb, Dorothy broke small pieces of bread off a loaf. She'd then roll them in her tiny palms until they became "pills" that she'd proudly present to her father to ease his discomfort. "Mmmmmm, delicious," Bill would say as he gobbled them down. In time, we all took her bread pills when we had an ailment. They were full of love and immensely healing.

Little Dorothy became Bill's youngest secretary, handling the job with equal parts zeal and uncommon efficiency. She'd walk

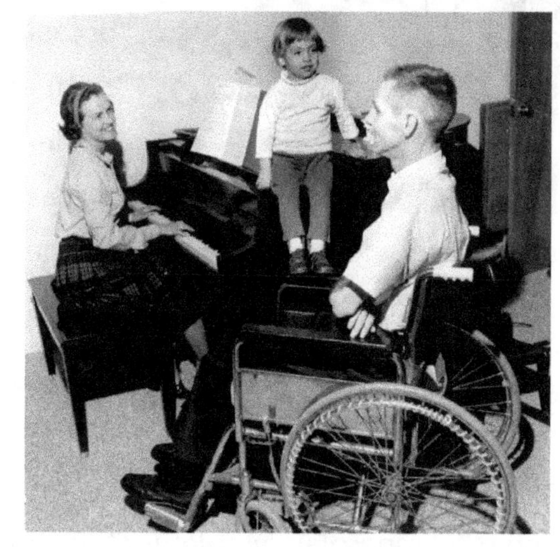

into his work area when there were no clients present with her child's toy typewriter and a blanket on which to park herself. She'd set up her blanket on the floor next to him, "typing" on papers he'd given her. She didn't want a desk. "I want to move my typewriter around," she'd say, as she put on a solemn business-like face. I wondered if I looked like that when I was typing. Probably so. She was always a good mimic.

Bill appointed himself as overseer of Dorothy's schoolwork. He hand-printed her times-tables up to twelve, each table printed individually on a letter-size piece of cardboard.

Sometimes Dorothy and I would watch television in the

bedroom, sitting on the bed with him sitting between us. I remember one particular occasion when Bill had his right arm around Dorothy and his left arm around me, giving us each an occasional light hug. Dorothy leaned over toward me and whispered, "It's like Christmas."

Throughout the years, of course, our children helped their father in their distinctive ways. When Jimmy was three, he and his father enjoyed playing their own kind of wrestling game. "Wanna play Monkeys?" Jimmy would ask, climbing all over his quite helpless father. Then suddenly, Bill would catch him with his right hand, and Jimmy would squeal with delight.

We attended Jimmy's baseball games all the way through high school. Bill was oftentimes the scorekeeper. He also oversaw Jimmy's schoolwork. Father and son spent countless hours writing catchy phrases for Jim's high school English contest with the hope they'd eventually be published in Reader's Digest.

"She was as pure as newly fallen snow until she drifted," was the one they held out the best hope for, but it didn't make the cut. Not that it mattered. What was evident was that Jimmy had inherited his father's wit.

I sometimes wondered why I was only five feet tall when I could have used a few more inches of height to get more leverage to more easily handle a wheelchair. I could manage up and down a curb, one step, but nothing higher. Once in a while, when Bill and I would be some place where we'd need help – if for example, an extra high curb had presented itself – we'd look for someone "tall" and with a friendly countenance. People were kind and almost always willing to give a hand.

We all had our own unique techniques of pushing Bill's wheelchair, identifiable to Bill without turning his head around to see who was pushing him

"Jim is the expert, the most self-confident when he's my pusher, but I love you all and you do good work too. Thank you," he'd say.

Bill's dedicated studying reached its end. He was one of the first quadriplegics in California to become a CPA. He was given two options to gain his final certification. He could either work for a CPA firm for two years, or he could work as a sole proprietor for ten years. Since it was much easier for him to work from home, he became a sole practitioner. Having a home office was good for me too, in part because I was reminded of my earlier sessions with Dr. Erickson. Then, ten years later on the dot, four qualified state examiners visited our home office to scrutinize Bill's work and evaluate his workplace. His final certification was never in question; nevertheless, the granting of it was celebratory and triumphant news to us, and it gave us an excuse to throw a great party.

We had lots of good friends, good food, good drinks, good music, and good fun. The party started at 4 o'clock in the afternoon, and we were still singing old songs at midnight while a Jesuit priest friend accompanied us on the piano. The music seemed to give us stamina, and we were all in good voice. Nobody wanted to stop – it was too enjoyable. Finally, our pianist quietly started to play, "Show me the way to go home. I'm tired and I wanna go to bed. …" We picked up the tune for a magnificent finale: a jubilant piano with spirited runs up and down the keyboard and us singing our hearts out in our very best style and in splendid harmony. We called it a great day and a great night. Bill's comment said it all, "The party was worth all the work it took to have a reason for the party." He nodded to me, "Right?" I'd been there through every inch of the way, and I double-nodded back. He threw me a kiss.

Several people phoned with thanks. I had often heard this in the past and now again was happy to hear, "You always have a great party." And this was true because those who came took on some of the responsibility for hospitality. Since Bill was unable to physically mop up a spilled drink or pour a cup of coffee, guests and our siblings would step in to keep things flowing. I always knew the reason guests had a great time. It was because they had given so much of themselves. And of course, I was grateful for their assistance.

Although we had our daily routines, we were free to make adjustments that served us best. Typically, after dressing Bill, I'd assist him in setting up his work for the day. Clients would come, or on some days Bill would travel to their place of business: a local dentist's office, a doctor's office, a market, a liquor store, a lumberyard, and the like. I, or a business student from nearby Loyola University, would be his driver. When Jimmy reached driving age, he also became one of his father's chauffeurs. Bill's three sisters and brother were gamely up for the task as well.

I was promoted from legal secretary to "office manager/accounting secretary," which meant I did a lot of typing. I didn't mind that. I was glad to be working in our business and in our home. I had learned by now that the freedom to make our own hours was a most welcomed gift.

Throughout the years after the accident, Bill's health often

necessitated visits to the hospital – for both short and long stays. Of course, we'd adjust our game plan accordingly and I would again find myself sitting at his bedside. When he was resting, or attending to visitors, I'd sit quietly and knit. The yarn silently moving through my hands and fingers mellowed

me. It was both enjoyable for me to knit and rewarding to create a sweater, a skirt, a shawl, or a pair of socks. Whether the finished garment was worn by another or me, it would remind me of where I was and what was happening in our lives at the time it was created. One of the favorite pieces I remember knitting was also Bill's favorite – an ivory sweater I gave him for his birthday. Bill knew it was going to be for him even before it was finished…and he insisted I add two pockets. I wasn't thrilled at the idea because pockets are a lot of work, but of course, in the end, the pockets, and Bill's wishes, prevailed.

What was always central for me, no matter where we were, was that Bill was my husband, my teacher, my lifelong friend, and the person I loved, admired, and respected most in this world. What was of super significance for me was that he listened to me with his whole heart. He was one of the best listeners I've ever known.

He remained a key decision-maker in our family. Of course we had our differences at times. After all, we had a lot to hash out. Did I ever think of just getting out of my situation? Yes, sometimes in the first few years when I'd get really tired and low. But that funk would pass in a few days, and in its place, I'd feel a kind of "conviction" that I belonged exactly where I was.

He thanked me a million times for being there. His compliments would sometimes take a bit of a twist, "You're the best wife I've ever had," or "I'd choose you again, you know."

I knew.

Bill was brilliant and fun. Not only was he an astute accountant, but he was also an insightful friend. Many of his business clients came to him for advice on personal issues. I could well understand that. He was always the first person I'd turn to for a usually unbiased, optimistic opinion.

*　　*　　*

It was during the first year and a half after his injury that I became acutely aware of how awkward some people felt in his presence, particularly when he was in the hospital. At one extreme, immediately after the accident, two of our friends were never to be seen again. The message they would send revealed their awkwardness, "We don't know what to say."

I wanted to say, "Just come--just show up--just be yourself. Your presence means a lot." But I didn't.

However, a seed had been planted then, and I now want to assist those who are reluctant, to help them reach a level of comfort so that they can support their own loved ones. I want them to recognize that simply their own presence is its own magical salve. For someone in the hospital, a visitor who is an unhurried listener is a bonus … and the visitor who understands the value of silence, a boon. Without words, without physical contact, patients absorb our presence and catch our vibe.

There were times when Bill would groan, "I find it difficult to be around people who want to share their ailments with me." Someone who is paralyzed, in a wheelchair, and cannot move himself is a captive audience. I've seen Bill captive and have also seen him get out of an uncomfortable encounter with a bit of humor or by deliberately changing the subject. I understood how patients must discover and apply fending tools.

A woman sitting a couple of rows ahead of us at a Hollywood Bowl concert one night kept constantly turning around to stare at Bill, sitting in his wheelchair. Finally, with a determined look on her face, she turned toward him again and shouted, "I beg your pardon, but what do you do when they play The Star-Spangled Banner?"

He called back, "I have a blanket pardon from the president."

"Oh," she gasped with relief, and turned away, satisfied.

I readily relied on Bill's ability to handle odd situations. He encouraged me with, "You can do it too, you know."

"Not as cleverly as you."

When Bill and I were out someplace together and were being introduced to someone, invariably that person would address his or her conversation initially to me. I would hesitate to speak, and Bill would quickly answer back. Nothing was intended against him, but it seemed to be natural for people to respond in this manner. I was comfortable, even at ease, at the way he included himself immediately.

Bill had a few strange months of being easily out-of-sorts. When he came out of it he was diagnosed with cancer in many areas of his body. His comment, "I'm feeling tired anyway," seemed to put the cap on his life.

Although I was devastated, within a short time I made a promise to myself to listen to everyone who came forward –

no matter how strange the suggestions might seem to me. I had lost my prejudices and my arrogance, and I read as many books as I could find on spiritual growth.

Bill questioned the books I was reading, and friction rose between us. He worried that if I kept on reading my faith – and his religion – would be compromised. So much of his strength, and certainly his belief in the perfection of the world and of life, reflected both his religious beliefs (especially those of the Jesuit priests he had studied with) and his character. I almost stopped reading. Then a nun, who was also our good friend, came to visit. When Bill mentioned his concern about my readings, she said, "Joyce must have a great thirst." I felt affirmed; someone recognized my need. I knew that in order for me to be the best I could be at this crucial time for Bill, the family, and myself, I needed to continue with my search even with Bill's strong disapproval. I couldn't stop, because I saw that it was the only way I could become stronger. After several months, I was stronger, and Bill noticed the difference when he surprisingly said to me one day, very quietly but with firm conviction, "You give me a lot of strength." As his cancer progressed, he grew to accept his death – an acceptance that took very little time, and he saw me, and my life's development, as a perfect part of the perfect whole. He was confident the family would be fine.

Many people phoned and asked to visit when they heard he was getting near to the end of his life. They found creative ways to help us: giving our daughter who was still so very young special attention, preparing meals for us, offering to do errands. A multitude of queries came our way asking, "What can I do to help you?" I felt cared about and cared for to a maximum.

One long-time good friend said, as he entered Bill's bedroom, "I know you don't need to see me, but I want to put my eyes on you."

So people came, selflessly following whatever directive was present that day, "Stay only a minute," or, "Sit down and have a cup of coffee."

Jimmy brought a delightful young woman to meet us. Bill had the opportunity to give them an approving nod, which turned out to be fortunate because he died before Jimmy and Cindy's marriage a year later.

Many individuals showed us a stunning example of caring. Those visitors who so generously opened their hearts enriched our family. They helped by giving us strength to assist Bill through his final days and also the strength to let him go.

And so it felt natural for me to be with Bill as he died. His brother Bob stopped by that night. Our son was also there with Cindy. She made a spaghetti dinner for everyone. Our daughter was in and out of Bill's room, coming in to give her father a tender pat. Our dog, Shadow, who had kept an on-

and-off vigil at his bedside for a day or so began to sit more steadily by the side of Bill's bed.

*   *   *

Bill died 26 years after the car accident. It was a long time to be immobile. I often wondered, and every now and then I'd ask him how he stood it. He'd shrug his shoulders, "It's my thing to do."

When friends prodded a little more and asked him, "How do you put up with being a quadriplegic?" I heard this answer, "At first I wondered 'Why me?' Then for a long time I wondered, 'Why anybody?' Then I looked at the universe, which I consider to be perfect, and I know if the universe is perfect, then I am a perfect part of it no matter what condition I'm in. I also know that there is a reason for my being paralyzed, and I don't yet have God's intelligence to understand why."

I have my own observations of Bill's life as I remember the Bill I first met and adored as impetuous, outgoing, Johnny-on-the-spot. He was quick to move, quick to do anything, always ahead of the game, though trustworthy and keen-minded. This was a lot to temper down, and it took him a while to rearrange his psyche. In a short time, his maturity, tenderness, and thoughtfulness would emerge and ultimately take the lead.

Thankfully, Bill made his own life, and ours, as rich as possible. He also made our life as easy as he could. Most of the time, he was a happy man. Most of the time, we were a happy family. Could there be a higher level of living than this?

Acknowledgements

It stuns me when I see the grace and caring Bill and I, and my family, received. Tears still flow. What follows may seem long and dry, but to me these "Givers" were as water in the desert. They are only a portion of those who reached out to us and who offered gracious assistance. Thank you:

To my parents, Jim and Corinne, and my brother, Billy, who played a major part in assisting us when Bill was first injured. We lived with them for seven years, and I never felt that we were in the way. They took care of our dear baby, Jimmy, and made their home "our home." It was no small order that they took on, and it touches my heart now even more as time goes on.

To Bill's parents, Bill and Mary Lea, and to his siblings, Marjorie, Dorothy, Bob, and Ginger, their spouses and offspring, who were always there for us … and who made sure we had a lot of laughs.

To all my aunts, uncles, and cousins, who never failed to stay in the picture and who enriched our lives. It was always so much fun to have them visit. Some lent me their car, some taught me how to ski, and each gave a helping hand.

To our children, Jim and Dorothy, who were a constant uplifting presence, and whom their father and I tenderly appreciated. And to our children's spouses, Cindy and Barney.

To my nieces and nephews, Marlene, Eileen, Lea, George, David, Mary, Shelly, Kevin, Rusty, David, Matthew, Janalea, Greg, Lynn, Kristen, Jennifer, and Mark who each gave a part of themselves to us with love and joy.

To Doctors Bors, Comar, and Barry at Long Beach Veterans Hospital who took consistently excellent care of Bill from the beginning of his injury and throughout the 26 years of his life, and who were generous with their time by answering all of my questions.

To our devoted bridge playing friends who kept the game going.

To our continuously helpful neighbors, the Kings and Kraemers in Manhattan Beach who invited everyone on the block over for a "clean up the yard" party" when we moved in.

To Loyola University Jesuits who kept in touch with Bill even when he discontinued his education with them.

To UCLA who remodeled their buildings so those who were in wheelchairs could attend. To all the professors who allowed us to sit in their offices and an assortment of odd places so Bill could dictate exam answers to me.

To the Certified Public Accountant testers who allowed us to sit within sight, but out of sound of the rest of those taking the CPA exams so Bill could dictate answers. Thanks also to the CPA supervisors and examiners who thoroughly scrutinized Bill's business ten years after he passed the exams in order to finalize his certification.

To our grandsons, Bill, Robby, Robert, and Dale, along with our great grandchildren, Jacob and Lilly, who readily offer love and support. They did not know their grandfather, Bill, yet have cared to learn about him and his fortitude.

To all those who kept encouraging me to write this book, Sunny, Kelly, Benetha, Maggie, Carole, Peggie, Rufina, Peg, Richard, Rocky, John, Donna, Darlene, Victoria, Shirley, Denise, Carol, Cherry, and Jane, et cetera, et cetera, et cetera.

To my teacher, Gurumayi Chidvilasananda, and her teacher, Baba Muktananda, who expanded my vision of life.

To the Siddha Yoga community for always being positive.

To Monsignor Deegan and Jack Flynn SJ, whose wisdom and love of life made a lasting impression.

To Caroline, Mary Lou, and my creative writing classmates who always gave valuable critiques.

To Landmark for sharing their fresh and amazing insights.

To those I haven't included, please know that I am grateful for your input in my life.

To Michele Nadder, who edited and saw into the essence of what I wanted to say in the book, and who supported and encouraged me with her patience (PATIENCE, editor's note). (Editor's second note: To Gatita, Michele's cat, who suffered her absence while she was editing Joyce's book.)

Icon made by Freepik from www.flaticon.com